Fun and Simple State Crafts

Fun and Simple
Southern
State Crafts

Kentucky, Tennessee, Alabama, Mississippi, Louisiana, and Arkansas

June Ponte

Enslow Elementary

an imprint of

Enslow Publishers, Inc.

40 Industrial Road
Box 398
Berkeley Heights, NJ 07922
USA

http://www.enslow.com

This book meets the National Council for the Social Studies standards.

Enslow Elementary, an imprint of Enslow Publishers, Inc.

Enslow Elementary® is a registered trademark of Enslow Publishers, Inc.

Library of Congress Cataloging-in-Publication Data

Ponte, June.
  Fun and simple Southern state crafts : Kentucky, Tennessee, Alabama, Mississippi, Louisiana, and Arkansas / June Ponte.
      p. cm. — (Fun and simple state crafts)
  Summary: "Provides facts and craft ideas for each of the states that make up the Southern region of the United States"—Provided by publisher.
  Includes bibliographical references and index.
  ISBN-13: 978-0-7660-2936-1
  ISBN-10: 0-7660-2936-0
  1. Handicraft—Southern States—Juvenile literature. I. Title.
  TT23.5.P652   2008
  745.50975—dc22
                                    2007014035

Printed in the United States of America

10 9 8 7 6 5 4 3 2 1

To Our Readers:
We have done our best to make sure all Internet Addresses in this book were active and appropriate when we went to press. However, the author and the publisher have no control over and assume no liability for the material available on those Internet sites or on other Web sites they may link to. Any comments or suggestions can be sent by e-mail to comments@enslow.com or to the address on the back cover.

Every effort has been made to locate all copyright holders of material used in this book. If any errors or omissions have occurred, corrections will be made in future editions of this book.

♻ Enslow Publishers, Inc., is committed to printing our books on recycled paper. The paper in every book contains 10% to 30% post-consumer waste (PCW). The cover board on the outside of each book contains 100% PCW. Our goal is to do our part to help young people and the environment too!

Illustration Credits: Crafts prepared by June Ponte; Photography by Nicole diMella/Enslow Publishers, Inc.; © 1999 Artville, LLC., pp. 6–7; © 2001 Robesus, Inc., all state flags. © Jupiterimages, pp. 9, 15, 21, 27, 33, 39.

Cover Illustration: Crafts prepared by June Ponte; Photography by Nicole diMella/Enslow Publishers, Inc.; © 1999 Artville, LLC., map; © Jupiterimages, state buttons.

CONTENTS

WELCOME TO THE SOUTHERN STATES!

Kentucky, Tennessee, Alabama, Mississippi, Louisiana, and Arkansas are the six states in the Southern region. The area is referred to as the South because these states are located in the southern area of the United States.

The geography of the Southern states is varied. The coastline of Alabama has many swamps and bayous. A bayou is a slow moving or swampy stream that flows from a larger river or lake. The southern area of Alabama has a coastal plain with rich black soil. The southern end of the Appalachian Mountains are in the northern part of the state.

In the northwestern area of Arkansas, the Ozark Plateau features steep ridges and low hills. Forests can be found in the lowlands of the southeastern part of Arkansas. In the hilly northwestern part of Kentucky, there are many large coal deposits.

The Bluegrass region, named for the tall, bright green grass in the area, is near the center of Kentucky. Black Mountain, the highest point in the state, can be found in the eastern part of Kentucky.

The great Mississippi River creates Louisiana's Delta area and flood plain. Swamps and bayous can be found along the coastline. In the northwest, hills can be found near the Red River. These are the highest points in the state. The Piney Woods are in southern Mississippi, along with coastal plains and meadow lands. Cypress trees grow in the Mississippi Delta region on the western side of the state.

Tennessee's geography is quite varied. The Great Smokey Range and the Great Appalachian Valley are in the eastern part of the state. The central part of the state features plateaus and wide basins. A plateau is a large area of high, flat land separated from the surrounding land by its steep edges. A basin is land which gradually descends to a river or a stream. Tennessee's western border is created by the Mississippi River.

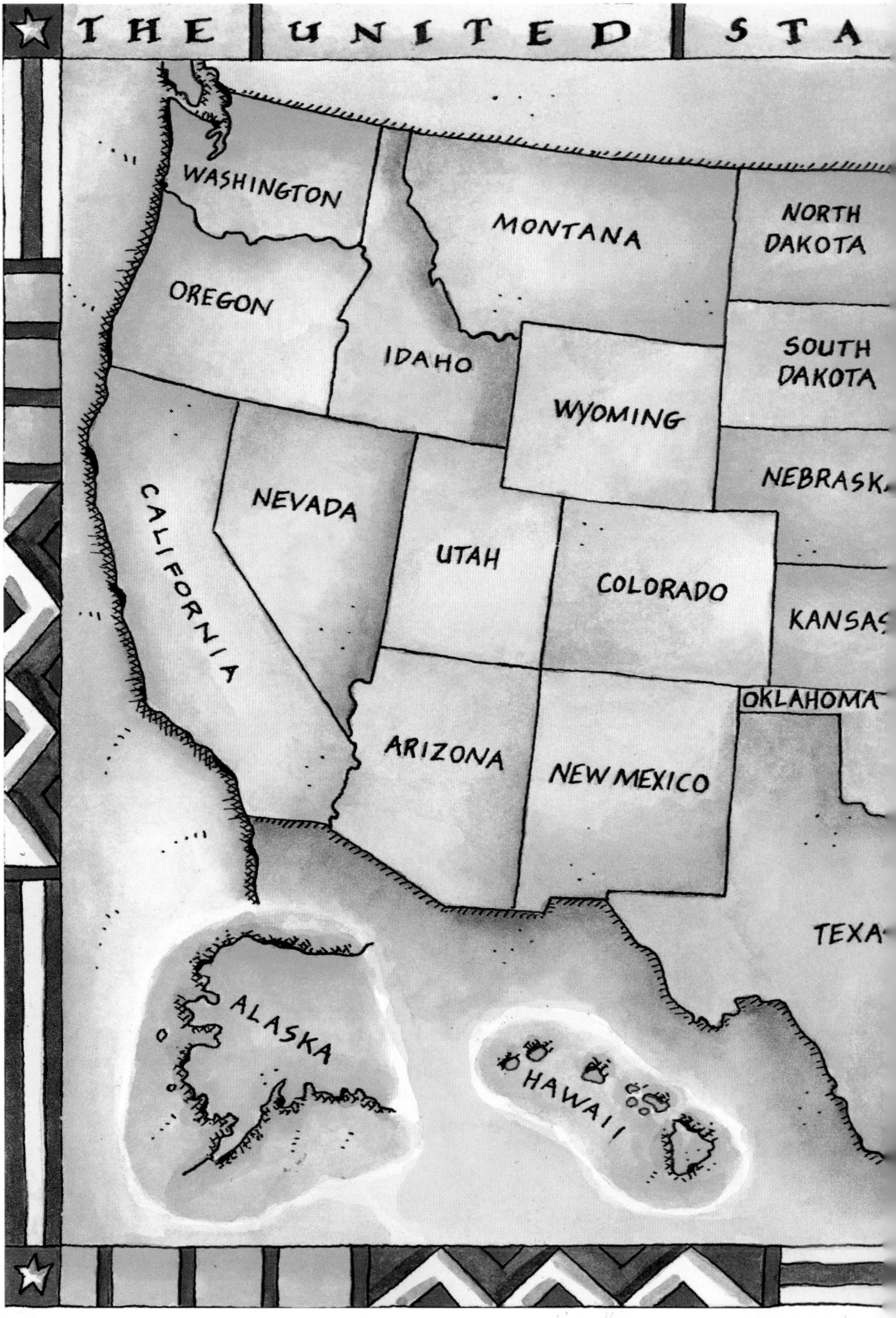
THE UNITED STA
WASHINGTON
OREGON
CALIFORNIA
IDAHO
MONTANA
NORTH DAKOTA
SOUTH DAKOTA
WYOMING
NEVADA
UTAH
COLORADO
NEBRASK
KANSAS
OKLAHOMA
ARIZONA
NEW MEXICO
TEXA
ALASKA
HAWAII

Southern States

KENTUCKY

Origin of name	Kentucky comes from the Iroquois Indian word *ken-tah-ten*, which means "land of tomorrow."
Flag	The Kentucky state flag is navy blue. In the center of the flag is a seal, surrounded by the words "Commonwealth of Kentucky." In the center of the seal, a statesman and pioneer are shaking hands. They represent Kentucky's motto, "United We Stand, Divided We Fall." Goldenrod, the state flower, is shown around the bottom of the seal.
Capital	Frankfort
Nickname	The Bluegrass State

Motto	"United We Stand, Divided We Fall"
Size (in area)	37th largest
Animal	grey squirrel
Bird	Kentucky cardinal
Fish	Kentucky bass
Flower	goldenrod
Tree	Kentucky coffeetree
Industry	car and truck manufacturing, chemical manufacturing, agriculture, coal mining, raising of horses

Mini Baseball Bat Pen

The Louisville Slugger Museum in Louisville, Kentucky, is a unique building. It has a giant 120-foot-tall baseball bat leaning on the side of the building! The company that owns the Louisville Slugger Museum makes the official bats for major league baseball players. It has been making wooden baseball bats since 1884.

What you will need

* terra cotta self-hardening clay
* stick pen
* tan poster paint
* paintbrush
* permanent markers
* glue wash
* paper bowl
* measuring cup

What you will do

1. Use a piece of self-hardening clay to form the shape of a bat around a stick pen. The point of the pen should be the handle of the bat, and left uncovered. Let dry.

2. Paint the clay tan. Let dry. Use a marker to write your name, or your favorite team's name on the bat.

3. Mix 1/8 cup of glue with 1/8 cup of water. Coat the bat with the glue wash. Let dry to a shiny finish.

USHABTIS MUMMY

The Speed Art Museum in Louisville is the oldest and biggest art museum in Kentucky. The museum's collection includes everything from ancient Egyptian art to the art of today. Ushabtis, figures of little Egyptian mummy gods, are part of the museum's collection. Ushabtis were found in ancient Egyptian tombs. These figures were thought to help the dead during the afterlife.

What you will need

* terra cotta self-hardening clay
* toothpick
* plastic knife
* cup of tea (ask permission first!)
* 1 foot of gauze
* white glue
* paintbrush
* tan, red, gold, and black poster paint

What you will do

1. Cut a piece of clay 4 inches x 1-1/2 inches. Flatten it to about 1/4 inch thick. With a toothpick, draw a mummy figure on the clay (See A). (See page 44 for the pattern.)

A)

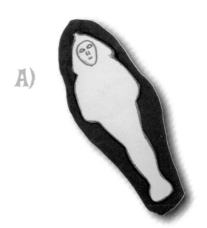

2. Use a toothpick to draw around the pattern into the clay. Remove the pattern, and use a plastic knife to cut out the mummy. Round off the sides with your fingers. Add two little pieces of clay to make the mummy's feet. Add eyes, a nose and a mouth on the face if you wish (See B). Let dry.

3. Ask an adult to make a cup of strong black tea. Place the piece of gauze in the tea for three hours. Remove and let dry.

B)

C)

4. Paint the mummy's head and feet with tan paint, and add details with red, black, and gold poster paint. Let dry.

5. Cut the gauze lengthwise into 1/4-inch-wide strips. Wrap around the clay mummy (See C). Do not cover the head or feet. Glue the end of the gauze.

TENNESSEE

Origin of name	The name Tennessee comes from the Cherokee word *tanasi*, which was the name of two villages on the Little Tennessee River.
Flag	Tennessee's state flag is red, with a white strip and a blue strip on the right. In the center are three stars within a blue circle. The stars represent the mountains, highlands, and lowlands of Tennessee.
Capital	Nashville
Nickname	The Volunteer State

Motto	"Agriculture and Commerce"
Size (in area)	36th largest
Animal	raccoon
Bird	mockingbird
Fish	Tennessee has two state fish, the channel bass and the smallmouth catfish.
Flower	iris
Tree	tulip poplar
Industry	agriculture, mining, livestock, chemicals

BUDDY PORTRAIT WITH BRAILLE

Morris Frank was a blind man who did not like to depend on others for help. A German shepherd dog named Buddy was trained in Switzerland by Dorothy Harrison Eustis for Morris Frank. Buddy became the first guide dog for the blind in the United States. With funds from Dorothy Harrison Eustis, Morris Frank created The Seeing Eye in Nashville. It was the first company to train dogs as guides for the blind.

What you will need

* pencil
* cream color poster board
* markers (optional)
* ruler
* black permanent marker

What you will do

1. Draw a picture of Buddy the German shepherd on the poster board. Draw a border around the edge of the picture.

2. Near the bottom of the poster board, draw two straight lines in pencil. They should be one under the other, across the page, about 1/2 inch apart. Press lightly into the poster board with the dull pencil to spell Buddy's name in braille. Turn the poster board over. With the dull pencil, press the dots so they will be raised on the other side.

3. Turn the poster board over and color in black dots over where the braille bumps are.

STOVEPIPE HAT PENNY BANK

The Abraham Lincoln Museum is in Harrowgate, Tennessee. It houses one of the largest collections of Abraham Lincoln and Civil War items. The museum has President Lincoln's silver-topped cane, a lock of his hair, and many other personal belongings. There are many photographs, paintings, and sculptures. Abraham Lincoln liked to wear a tall, black, stovepipe hat.

What you will need

* scissors
* toilet tissue tube
* black felt
* white glue
* cardboard
* ruler
* poster board
* red construction paper
* gold metallic marker
* glitter pen

What you will do

1. Cut 3 inches off a toilet tissue tube. Cut a piece of black felt to fit around the tube. Cover the tube with white glue. Place the felt over the glue to cover the tube (See A). Let dry.

A)

2. Cut a circle out of cardboard that is 1 inch larger than a opening of the tube. Glue it to a piece of felt and let dry. Cut off the excess felt. Glue the felt-covered circle, face up, onto one end of the tube. Let dry.

B)

3. Trace the other end of the tube onto poster board. Cut out the circle. Cut a 1 inch x 1/4 inch slot in the center. Glue the circle to black felt. Let dry. Cut off the excess felt. Carefully cut through the hole to make a slot in the felt. Glue the circle to the top of the tube (See B). Let dry.

4. Cut a strip of red construction paper about 1/4 inch wide. Make it long enough to go around the tube and overlap a little. Write "President Lincoln" with a gold metallic marker. Let dry. Glue it around the bottom of the hat near the brim (See C). Let dry.

C)

ALABAMA

Origin of name	The name Alabama is thought to come from a Choctaw American Indian phrase which means "plant gatherer."
Flag	The Alabama state flag is white with a red cross on it. It was designed after the Confederate Battle Flag that was used during the United States Civil War.
Capital	Montgomery
Nickname	The Camellia State and The Heart of Dixie
Motto	*Audemus Jura Nostra Defendere* (This is a Latin sentence which means "We dare defend our rights.")

Size (in area)	30th largest
Animal	racking horse
Bird	yellowhammer
Fish	Alabama has two state fish, the saltwater tarpon and the freshwater largemouth bass
Flower	camellia
Tree	southern longleaf pine
Industry	soybeans, nuts, fruits, vegetables, poultry, beef, dairy, steel, textiles, chemicals

ROSA PARKS QUOTE PLAQUE

In 1955, racial segregation existed in Alabama. Segregation is separating people by their race.

What you will need

* alphabet pasta
* gold metallic poster paint
* 50 inches each of green, black, and red ribbon
* scissors
* ruler
* white glue
* 11-inch x 14-inch green poster board
* marker
* clear tape
* 20 inches of ribbon or yarn

African Americans were not allowed to drink from the same water fountains as white people. African Americans had to give up their seat on a bus if a white person wanted it.

In 1955, Rosa Parks, an African-American woman, would not give up her seat for a white passenger. Her courage inspired many positive changes for African Americans. Rosa Parks is called "the Mother of the Modern Civil Rights Movement." An important quote to remember by Rosa Parks is: "To this day I believe we are here on the planet Earth to live, grow up, and do what we can to make this world a better place for all people to enjoy freedom." Today, there is a library and museum in Alabama dedicated to Rosa Parks.

What you will do

A)

1. Choose the pasta letters you will need for the Rosa Parks quote. Paint the pasta letters using gold metallic paint (See A). Let dry.

2. Cut the green ribbon into two 11-inch pieces and two 14-inch pieces. Repeat, using the black and red ribbon (See B). Glue the red ribbon along the edges of the green poster board. Below the red ribbon, glue the black ribbon. Repeat with the green ribbon. Let the corners overlap (See C). Let dry.

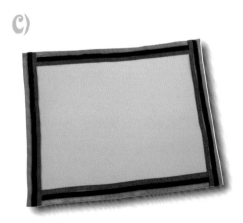

B)

3. Glue the painted letters, spelling out Rosa Parks' quote on the poster board. Let dry. If you wish, use a marker to draw a design. Tape ribbon to the back of the poster board and display (See D).

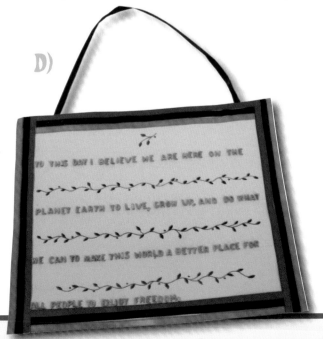

D)

C)

MARDI GRAS BEADED CROWN

The Mardi Gras Cottage Museum in Mobile, Alabama, has many fascinating artifacts from Mardi Gras celebrations of long ago. Mardi Gras means Fat Tuesday, a festival that precedes Ash Wednesday. This day marks the start of Lent, a time of fasting and prayer before Christians celebrate Easter. People celebrate Mardi Gras with parades, costume balls, and carnivals.

What you will need

* scissors
* yellow poster board
* pencil
* hole punch
* white glue
* pipe cleaners
* glitter
* markers
* plastic beads
* ribbon or yarn

Mobile has been celebrating Mardi Gras for more than three hundred years. Mardi Gras celebrations usually take place in February or early March.

What you will do

1. Cut a strip of yellow poster board 6 inches wide and 20 inches long (See A).

A)

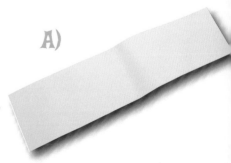

Fold the strip in half. With the poster board folded, draw a Mardi Gras crown on one side of the poster board (See page 46 for the pattern). Cut out along the top edge of the crown (See B). Unfold. Punch a hole in each end of the crown.

B)

2. Glue colorful pipe cleaners and beads onto the crown. Fill in areas of the crown with glitter. Color other areas with marker. Let dry. Glue on plastic beads (See C). Let dry.

3. Cut two 8-inch pieces of yarn or ribbon and thread one piece through each hole at the ends of the crown. Tie a knot near each hole. Place the crown on your head and tie it so that the crown fits well.

C)

MISSISSIPPI

Origin of name	The state of Mississippi received its name from the American Indian word meaning "great river."
Flag	The Mississippi state flag has three stripes of navy blue, white, and red. In the top left corner is the union square, or Confederate battle flag. It is red and has thirteen five-pointed white stars in a blue cross.
Capital	Jackson
Nickname	The Magnolia State

Motto	*Virtute et Armis* (This is a Latin phrase which means "by valor and arms.")
Size (in area)	32nd largest
Animal	white-tailed deer
Bird	mockingbird
Fish	largemouth bass
Flower	magnolia
Tree	magnolia
Industry	tourism, poultry, livestock, paper and textile manufacturing

MAD POTTERY BOWL

George Ohr was a very creative potter. He was born in Biloxi, Mississippi, in 1857. He was known for his playful spirit and called himself "The Mad Potter of Biloxi." His pottery was made in unusual shapes. A museum to show Ohr's art was being built in 2005, when Hurricane Katrina hit. The building was destroyed. It will be rebuilt and feature the work of George Ohr.

What you will need

* self-hardening clay
* pencil
* poster paint
* paintbrush
* glue wash
* paper bowl
* measuring cup

What you will do

1. Roll a piece of clay until it is soft and easy to work with. Make a ball that is about 4 inches wide.

2. Press into the center of the ball with your thumb. Keep pushing around the sides of the clay until you have formed a bowl shape.

3. Push or pull the sides of the clay bowl to make an unusual shape. Add clay shapes to the bowl. Blend the clay together where it meets the bowl. Poke holes in the clay with a pencil around the top edge or bottom to make an openwork design. Let dry.

4. Paint the bowl. Let dry. Mix 1/8 cup of glue with 1/8 cup of water. Coat the bowl with the glue wash. Let dry for a shiny finish.

PETRIFIED FOREST

The Mississippi Petrified Forest is in Flora, Mississippi. The petrified wood is 36 million years old. The logs were left in the area by a raging river. Petrified wood is wood that minerals have seeped into over time. The minerals replace the original wood with rock, creating petrified wood.

What you will need

* blue poster board
* paintbrush
* poster paint
* white glue
* brown pipe cleaners
* twigs
* yarn
* ruler
* scissors
* clear tape

What you will do

1. Paint a sun, clouds, and grass on a piece of poster board. Let dry.

2. Glue brown pipe cleaners around the edge of the poster board. Glue the twigs on the poster board to make a forest. Let dry.

3. Tape a 14 inch piece of yarn on the back of the poster board.

LOUISIANA

Origin of name	Louisiana was named after the French ruler, Louis XIV. He was the king of France from 1643 to 1715.
Flag 	The Louisiana state flag is blue. A group of pelicans taken from the state seal, is shown in the center of the flag in white and gold. A white banner with the state motto, "Union, Justice and Confidence," is shown below.
Capital	Baton Rouge
Nickname	The Pelican State

Motto	"Union, Justice and Confidence"
Size (in area)	31st largest
Animal	black bear
Bird	Eastern brown pelican
Fish	white perch
Flower	magnolia
Tree	bald cypress
Industry	petrochemicals, tourism, gaming

FOLK ART DOLLS

There are many talented folk artists in Louisiana. Many of these artists are American Indian and African-American. Some folk artists make wonderful dolls that reflect their heritage. The artists use many different things to make their dolls, from colorful bits of fabric to corn husks.

What you will need

* pen
* felt in many colors
* scissors
* yarn
* white glue
* 4 medium-sized wiggle eyes
* dry lentils or dry split peas
* cotton balls
* fabric scrap (optional)
* buttons or beads (optional)
* pipe cleaner (optional)

A)

What you will do

1. Draw a boy and girl shape on felt. (See page 45 for the patterns.) Cut out the shapes. Draw around the shapes on another piece of felt. Cut them out. You will have two shapes for each doll (See A).

2. Cut pieces of yarn to use as hair. Cut the yarn long for the girl doll and short for the boy doll. Glue the yarn to the heads and let dry (See B).

3. Glue wiggle eyes to each doll's face. Cut out two small felt triangles. Glue one on each doll for the nose. Let dry. Glue dry lentils or dry split peas to form a mouth on each doll (See C). Let dry.

B)

4. Glue the two doll halves together around the edge, leaving the head unglued. Let dry. Stuff with cotton balls. Glue the rest of the head closed. Repeat with the second doll. If you wish, use fabric scrap, buttons, and pipe cleaners to dress your doll and add details (See D). (See page 46 for the patterns).

C)

D)

JUMPING FROG

The annual Frog Festival takes place on Labor Day weekend in Rayne, Louisiana. For more than thirty years, a world championship frog racing and jumping contest has been held there. Thousands of people come to the festival each year to see the frogs race.

What you will need

* pencil
* poster board
* scissors
* poster paint
* paintbrush
* white glue
* beads

What you will do

1. Using a pencil, draw a frog on poster board, and cut it out. (See page 46 for the pattern.) Draw a 1-inch x 3-inch rectangle on the poster board, and cut out. Fold the poster board into three sections.

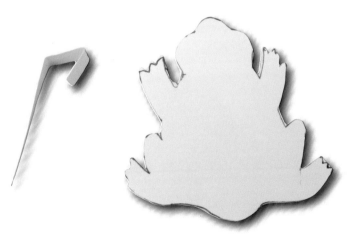

2. Paint the frog bright green, with orange or red designs. Let dry. Glue on beads for eyes and let dry.

3. Turn the frog over. Glue one section of the folded poster board onto the center of the frog. Let dry.

4. Turn the frog over and press down gently. Release the frog and watch him jump!

ARKANSAS

Origin of name	Arkansas means "south wind" in the Quapaw American Indian language.
Flag 	The Arkansas state flag is red with a diamond shape outlined with white stars in a blue border. The diamond shape represents the fact that Arkansas is the only place in North America where the discovery and mining of diamonds took place. The twenty-five white stars in the border of the diamond show that Arkansas was the twenty-fifth state to join the union. The top blue stars in the center represent Arkansas membership as one of the Confederate States during the Civil War. Spain, the United States, and France are represented by the other three blue stars. These countries had once ruled the area that included Arkansas.

Capital	Little Rock
Nickname	The Land of Opportunity
Motto	*Regnat Populus* (This is a Latin phrase which means "The People Rule.")
Size (in area)	29th largest
Bird	mockingbird
Animal	white-tailed deer
Insect	honeybee
Flower	apple blossom
Tree	pine tree
Industry	agriculture, lumber, shipbuilding, cotton, manufacturing

ALLIGATOR CANDY BOX

The Arkansas Alligator Farm in Hot Springs was founded in 1902. Here you can see more than two hundred alligators. Some of them are only twelve inches long, and some are twelve feet long! When baby alligators hatch from their eggs, they are only about six inches long. Alligators grow nearly one foot each year. They have about eighty teeth. Alligators are carnivores. A carnivore is a meat-eater, but an alligator will take a taste of almost anything it finds. That includes rocks, aluminum cans, sticks, and more!

What you will need

* pencil
* green craft foam
* scissors
* white glue
* 2 wiggle eyes
* white paper
* permanent markers
* glitter pen
* small box, such as a square tissue box
* individually wrapped candies

What you will do

1. Draw an alligator head, body, and legs on green craft foam (See A). (See page 44 for the pattern.) Cut out all the parts.

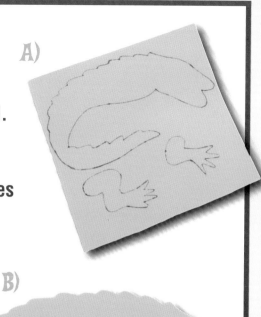

2. Glue the legs onto the body of the alligator (See B). Let dry. Glue the wiggle eyes onto the alligator's head. Let dry.

3. For the teeth, cut out 6 small triangles of white paper. Glue them to the top and bottom of the alligator's mouth (See C). Let dry.

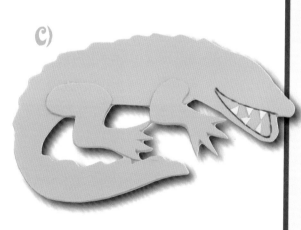

4. Use markers and a glitter pen to add details to the alligator such as toes, a mouth, and a ridge on his tail. Glue the alligator to the front of the box (See D). Fill the box with candies.

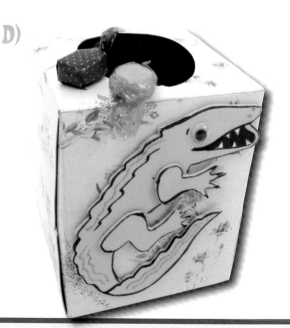

NODENA RED AND WHITE POTTERY

In the town of Wilson, Arkansas, a fifteen-acre farming village was unearthed. From about 1350 to 1700 the ancestors of the Chickasaw lived there. More than seven hundred pieces of pottery, called Nodena red and white pottery, were discovered in the village.

What you will need

* terra cotta self-hardening clay
* red and white poster paint
* paintbrush

What you will do

1. Roll out a piece of clay until it is about 1/2 inch thick and 20 inches long (See A).

2. Coil the clay to make a piece of pottery (See B). Choose any shape you like.

A)

3. Smooth the coiled areas of clay together to make an even surface.

B)

4. Roll or press a 1/4-inch-thick flat piece of clay. Make it the right shape to fit the bottom of your piece of pottery (See C). Smooth the top and bottom of the clay pieces together. Let dry.

5. Paint the pottery half red and half white (See D). Let dry.

C)

D)

PATTERNS

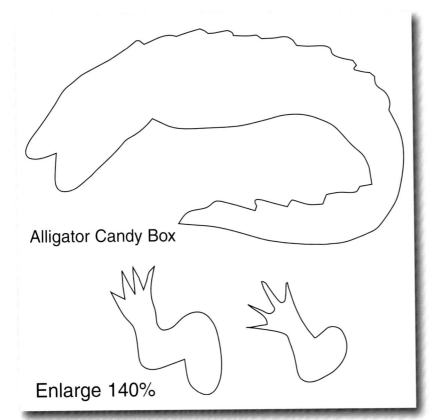

Alligator Candy Box

Enlarge 140%

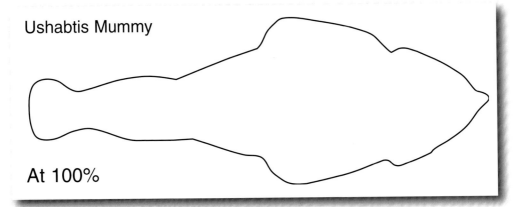

Ushabtis Mummy

At 100%

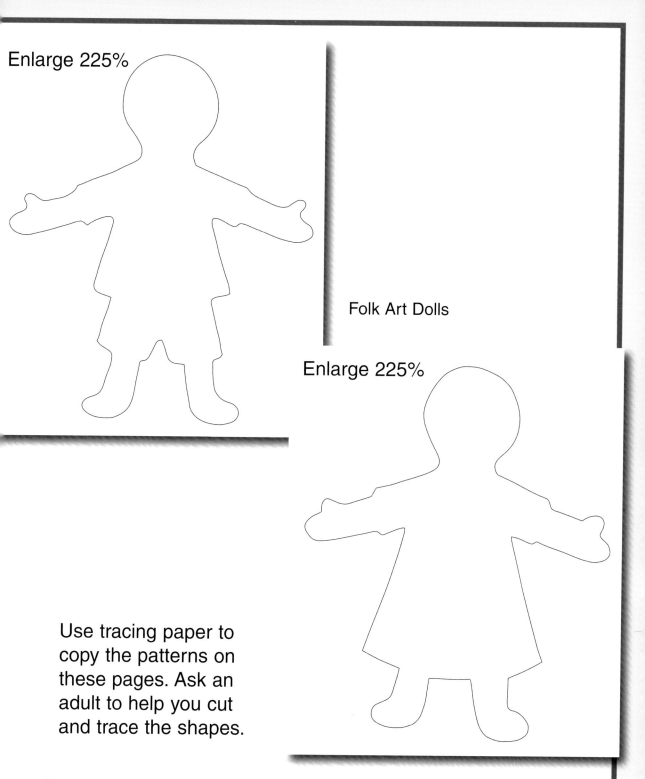

Enlarge 225%

Folk Art Dolls

Enlarge 225%

Use tracing paper to copy the patterns on these pages. Ask an adult to help you cut and trace the shapes.

Mardi Gras Beaded Crown

Enlarge 220%

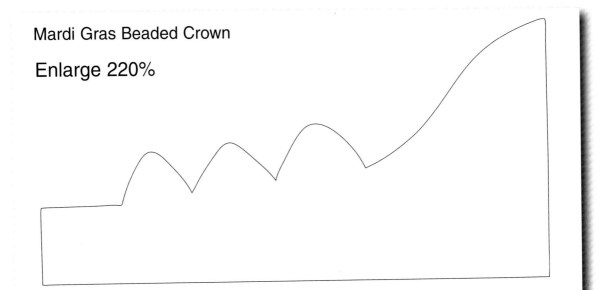

Enlarge 145%

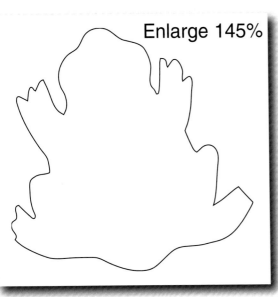

Jumping Frog

Folk Art Doll Clothes

Enlarge 215%

LEARN MORE

Books

Corwin, Jeff. *Into Wild Louisiana.* San Diego, Calif.: Blackbirch Press, 2004.

Hart, Joyce. *Alabama.* New York: Marshall Cavendish Benchmark, 2006.

Heinrichs, Ann. *Kentucky.* Chanhassen, Minn.: Child's World, 2006.

Heinrichs, Ann. *Mississippi.* Minneapolis, Minn.: Compass Point Books, 2004.

Murray, Julie. *Arkansas.* Buddy Books, 2005.

Petreycik, Rick. *Tennessee.* New York: Marshall Cavendish Benchmark, 2006.

Internet Addresses

50states.com
<http://www.50states.com/>

U.S. States
<http://www.enchantedlearning.com/usa/states/>

INDEX